self care

This journal belongs to

_____

Dedication

This journal is dedicated to children and the youth. Love starts with YOU. Loving yourself is essential to a happy life. Taking care of yourself is key to being consistent and successful in life.

MORNING CHECK IN

I WOKE UP FEELING

Awesome   Good   Okay   Not good   Horrible

What do you want to accomplish today?

_____

_____

_____

_____

How do you want to feel today?

_____

_____

_____

_____

Today's affirmation:

_____

Morning Mind starter

Date

Pray/Mediate

Smile

Keep it positive

Aa...

I am awesome.

List one thing that is awesome about YOU.

_____

_____

_____

_____

_____

_____

_____

_____

_____

_____

_____

Bb...

I am brave.

List one thing that makes YOU brave.

_____

_____

_____

_____

_____

_____

_____

_____

_____

_____

_____

Cc...

I am capable.

List one thing that YOU are capable of doing.

_____

_____

_____

_____

_____

_____

_____

_____

_____

_____

_____

Dd...

I am determined.

List one thing that YOU are determined to achieve.

_____

_____

_____

_____

_____

_____

_____

_____

_____

_____

Ee...

I am elegant.

What makes YOU elegant?

_____

_____

_____

_____

_____

_____

_____

_____

_____

_____

Ff...

I am **fierce** and fearless.

Draw a picture of yourself or paste a picture of YOU showing your fierceness.

Gg...

I am **golden** and **great**.

Do you see the ☀ sunlight at the end of the tunnel?

What have YOU been working on and shining gracefully?

_____

_____

_____

_____

_____

_____

_____

_____

_____

_____

Hh...

I am honest.

How do YOU feel when you are transparent with others?

_____

_____

_____

_____

_____

_____

_____

_____

_____

_____

Ii...

I am important.

How do YOU present yourself to others?

_____

_____

_____

_____

_____

_____

_____

_____

_____

_____

_____

Jj...

I am joyful.

What makes YOU feel joyful?

_____

_____

_____

_____

_____

_____

_____

_____

_____

_____

Kk...

I am kind.

Think about a time when YOU were kind to yourself and a time when you were kind to someone. How did it make YOU feel?

_____

_____

_____

_____

_____

_____

_____

_____

_____

_____

Ll...

I am loved.

Explain how YOU express gratitude to your loved ones.

_____

_____

_____

_____

_____

_____

_____

_____

_____

_____

_____

Mm..
I am magnificent.

_____

_____

_____

_____

_____

_____

_____

_____

_____

_____

_____

Nn...

I am natural.

How do YOU embrace your authentic self?

_____

_____

_____

_____

_____

_____

_____

_____

_____

_____

_____

Oo...

I am open-minded.

What have YOU discovered recently?

_____

_____

_____

_____

_____

_____

_____

_____

_____

_____

_____

Pp...

I am peaceful.

How do you maintain your peace?

_____

_____

_____

_____

_____

_____

_____

_____

_____

_____

_____

Qq...
I am qualified.

What are your skills, and/or talents?

_____

_____

_____

_____

_____

_____

_____

_____

_____

_____

Rr...

I am relaxed.

What are some ways you rest your mind and body?

_____

_____

_____

_____

_____

_____

_____

_____

_____

_____

Ss...

I am strong

What are your values? Explain how you stand true to them.

_____

_____

_____

_____

_____

_____

_____

_____

_____

_____

Tt...

I am thriving.

Make a list of 2-3 areas you have developed and are doing well.

_____

_____

_____

_____

_____

_____

_____

_____

_____

_____

_____

Uu...

I am unique and unstoppable.

What makes you different from others?

_____

_____

_____

_____

_____

_____

_____

_____

_____

_____

Vv...

I am vibrant and vocal.

Write about a time you advocated for yourself.

_____

_____

_____

_____

_____

_____

_____

_____

_____

_____

_____

Ww...

I am worthy.

Share something you did today or this week that made you feel good or proud.

_____

_____

_____

_____

_____

_____

_____

_____

_____

_____

Xx...

I am the x-factor.

_____

_____

_____

_____

_____

_____

_____

_____

_____

_____

_____

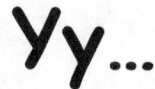

Yy...

I am yearning to reach my goals.
List at least two goals you are working on to
fulfill this year.

_____

_____

_____

_____

_____

_____

_____

_____

_____

_____

Zz...

I am zealous.

What are you passionate about?

_____

_____

_____

_____

_____

_____

_____

_____

_____

_____

_____

Glossary:

Awesome- extremely impressive; inspiring great admiration.

Brave- showing courage.

Capable- having the ability, fitness, or quality necessary to achieve a specified thing.

Determined- having made a firm decision and being resolved not to change it.

Elegant- pleasingly graceful and stylish in appearance or manner.

Fierce- having or displaying an intense or ferocious aggressiveness.

Golden- colored or shining like gold.

Honest- free of deceit and untruthfulness; sincere.

Important- of great significance or value.

Joyful- feeling or causing great pleasure and happiness.

Kind- a group of people or things having similar characteristics.

Loved- feel deep affection for

Magnificent- impressively beautiful, elaborate, or extravagant;

Natural- not made or caused by humankind

Open-minded- the readiness to consider something without prejudice.

Peaceful- free from disturbance; tranquil.

Qualified: be authorized or to get through

Radiant- sending out light; shining or glowing brightly.

Spectacular- beautiful in a dramatic and eye-catching way.

Thrive- prosper; flourish

Unique- being the only one of its kind; unlike anything else.

Unstoppable- impossible to stop or prevent.

Vibrant- full of energy and enthusiasm.

Worthy- having the qualities or abilities that merit recognition in a specified way.

X-factor- a noteworthy special talent or quality.

Yearning- a feeling of intense longing for something.

Zeal- great energy or enthusiasm in pursuit of a cause or an objective.

Zealous- showing great energy or enthusiasm in pursuit of a cause or objective.

Weekly check in

DATE _____

TOP 3 THINGS I DID THIS WEEK

○ _____

○ _____

○ _____

THIS WEEK I FELT

MOST REWARDING INTERACTION I HAD THIS WEEK

NEXT WEEK I WANT TO _____

_____

_____

_____

_____

THINGS I ACCOMPLISHED THIS WEEK

WHAT WAS THE BEST THING ABOUT THE WEEK?

MY RANKING OF THE WEEK

☆ ☆ ☆ ☆ ☆

Weekly check in

DATE _____

TOP 3 THINGS I DID THIS WEEK _____

○ _____

○ _____

○ _____

MOST REWARDING INTERACTION I
HAD THIS WEEK _____

THIS WEEK I FELT _____

NEXT WEEK I WANT TO _____

_____

_____

_____

_____

THINGS I ACCOMPLISHED THIS
WEEK _____

WHAT WAS THE BEST THING
ABOUT THE WEEK? _____

MY RANKING OF THE WEEK _____

☆ ☆ ☆ ☆ ☆

Weekly check in

DATE _____

TOP 3 THINGS I DID THIS WEEK
- ○ _____
- ○ _____
- ○ _____

THIS WEEK I FELT

NEXT WEEK I WANT TO _____

_____

_____

_____

_____

THINGS I ACCOMPLISHED THIS WEEK _____

MOST REWARDING INTERACTION I HAD THIS WEEK

WHAT WAS THE BEST THING ABOUT THE WEEK?

MY RANKING OF THE WEEK
☆ ☆ ☆ ☆ ☆

Weekly check in

DATE _____

TOP 3 THINGS I DID THIS WEEK _____

○ _____

○ _____

○ _____

MOST REWARDING INTERACTION I HAD THIS WEEK _____

THIS WEEK I FELT _____

NEXT WEEK I WANT TO _____

_____

_____

_____

_____

THINGS I ACCOMPLISHED THIS WEEK _____

WHAT WAS THE BEST THING ABOUT THE WEEK? _____

MY RANKING OF THE WEEK _____

☆ ☆ ☆ ☆ ☆

6 Minute Gratitude Journal

__/__/___

S M T W TH F S

Breath before writing

INHALE EXHALE INHALE EXHALE INHALE EXHALE

Things you're grateful today

* _____
* _____
* _____
* _____
* _____

3 best thing about today

Describe today in a drawing

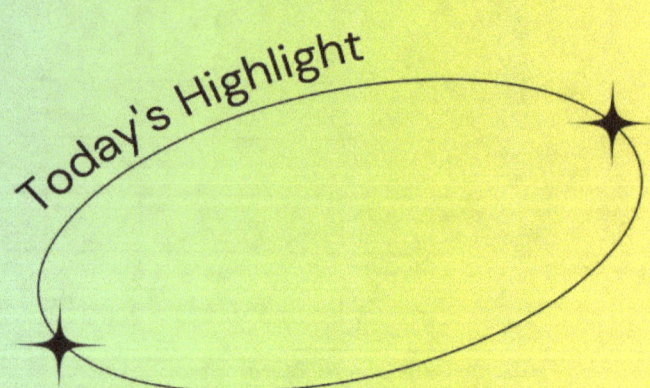

Today's Highlight

Things that you learned

_____
_____
_____
_____

Today's Affirmation

_____
_____

6 Minute Gratitude Journal

__/__/___

S M T W TH F S

Breath before writing

INHALE EXHALE INHALE EXHALE INHALE EXHALE

Things you're grateful today

* _____
* _____
* _____
* _____
* _____

3 best thing about today

Today's Highlight

Describe today in a drawing

Things that you learned

_____
_____
_____
_____

Today's Affirmation

_____
_____

6 Minute Gratitude Journal

Breath before writing

INHALE EXHALE INHALE EXHALE INHALE EXHALE

3 best thing about today

Things you're grateful today

✳ _____
✳ _____
✳ _____
✳ _____
✳ _____

Describe today in a drawing

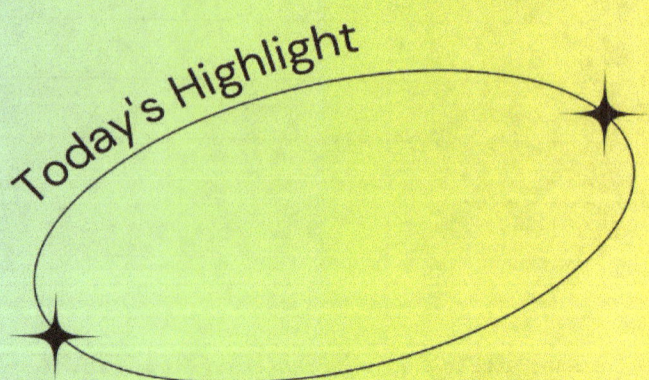

Today's Highlight

Things that you learned

_____
_____
_____
_____

Today's Affirmation

_____
_____

 Minute Gratitude Journal

__/__/___

S M T W TH F S

Breath before writing

INHALE EXHALE INHALE EXHALE INHALE EXHALE

Things you're grateful today

* _____
* _____
* _____
* _____
* _____

Describe today in a drawing

Today's Affirmation

_____

_____

3 best thing about today

Today's Highlight

Things that you learned

_____

_____

_____

_____

GOAL TRACKER

Goal 1:

Start Date

End Date

My Why

Action Steps
○
○
○
○

Notes

Goal 2:

Start Date

End Date

My Why

Action Steps
○
○
○
○

Notes

Goal 3:

Start Date

End Date

My Why

Action Steps
○
○
○
○

Notes

Goal 4:

Start Date

End Date

My Why

Action Steps
○
○
○
○

Notes

GOAL TRACKER

Goal 1:

Start Date

End Date

My Why

Action Steps

○
○
○
○

Notes

Goal 2:

Start Date

End Date

My Why

Action Steps

○
○
○
○

Notes

Goal 3:

Start Date

End Date

My Why

Action Steps

○
○
○
○

Notes

Goal 4:

Start Date

End Date

My Why

Action Steps

○
○
○
○

Notes

GOAL TRACKER

Goal 1:

Start Date

Action Steps

Notes

End Date

○

My Why

○

○

○

Goal 2:

Start Date

Action Steps

Notes

End Date

○

My Why

○

○

○

Goal 3:

Start Date

Action Steps

Notes

End Date

○

My Why

○

○

○

Goal 4:

Start Date

Action Steps

Notes

End Date

○

My Why

○

○

○

GOAL TRACKER

Goal 1:

Start Date

End Date

My Why

Action Steps

○
○
○
○

Notes

Goal 2:

Start Date

End Date

My Why

Action Steps

○
○
○
○

Notes

Goal 3:

Start Date

End Date

My Why

Action Steps

○
○
○
○

Notes

Goal 4:

Start Date

End Date

My Why

Action Steps

○
○
○
○

Notes

Evening Gratitude

2 things I'm grateful for today are...

_____

_____

_____

The best part of today was...

_____

_____

_____

What can I learn from today's experiences?

_____

_____

_____

Tomorrow I'm excited and looking forward to...

_____

_____

_____

You accomplish more with positive energy.

Self-Care
Tips

→ Pray/say daily affirmations

Explore something new ←

→ Take walk or jog

Journal your thoughts ←

→ Take a nap

Listen to music ←

keep it Positive

Letter to your future self

Dear _____

_____

_____

_____

_____

_____

_____

_____

_____

_____

_____

_____

_____

_____

_____

_____

_____

_____

_____

_____

Message from the Author:

Life is a journey. Make the best of it with your mind and actions. Preserve your energy. Surround yourself with positivity and uplifting thoughts. Be in a group you can learn from and pour into. Always think before you react!

Tip: Be still, listen, reflect then react effectively.

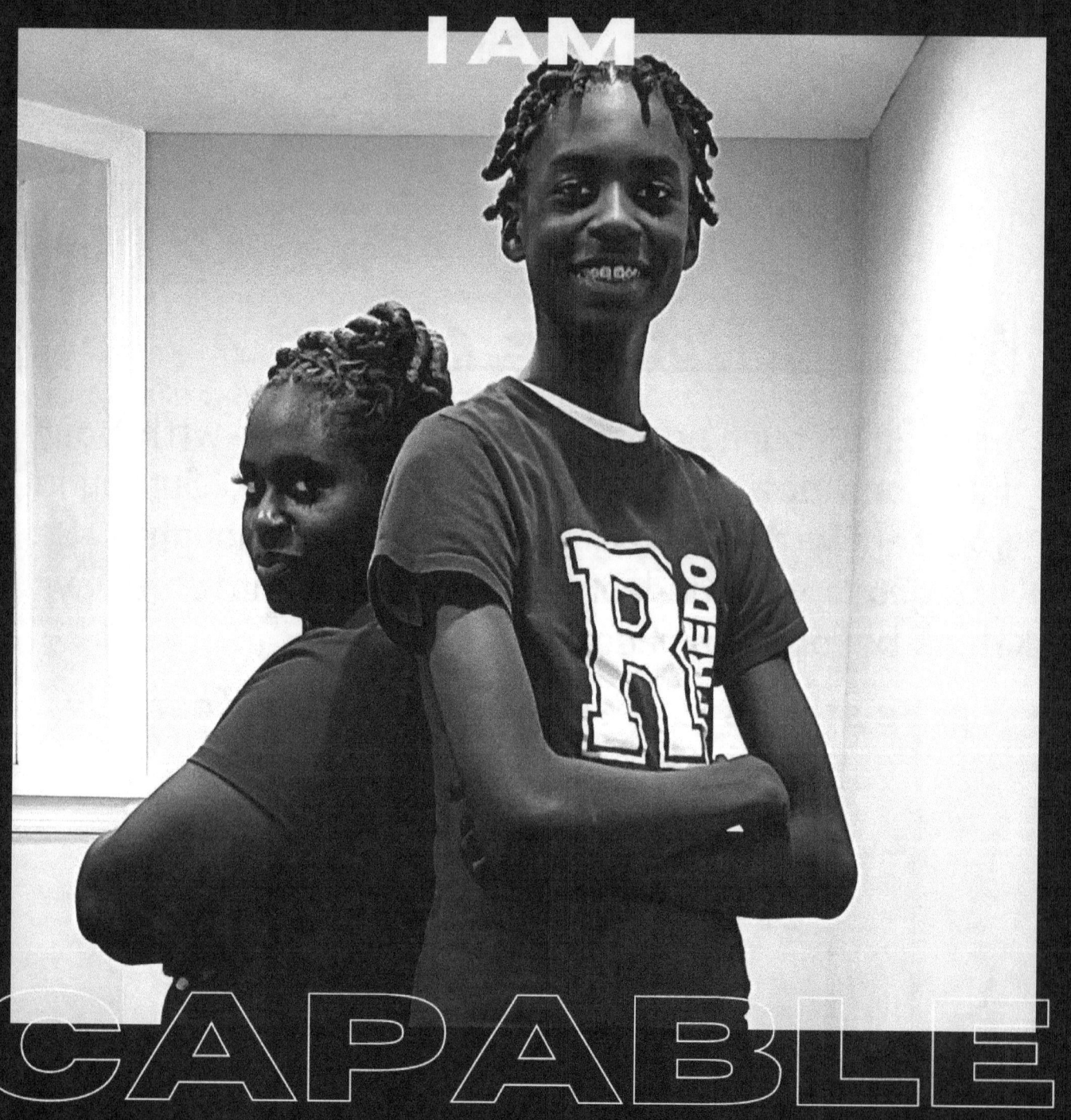